# The Surname Sparke

## Susan Morris &
## Wendy Bosberry-Scott

The question of surnames, their origins, distribution and history, lies at the heart of genealogy as well as being fascinating in its own right.

In the 1980s and 1990s, long before many genealogical sources were even indexed, let alone online, our Surname Report service provided expert assessments of the origins, history and distribution of selected British surnames, using the sources available at the time.

Now, with so many more sources available, we believe that these reports retain their value as studies of individual surnames, and so we are gradually making the Debrett Surname Archive available online and in print for the first time. Some modern indexes have been consulted to refresh and update the reports.

Debrett Ancestry Research Ltd, PO Box 379,
Winchester SO23 9YQ
Tel: 01962 841904
Email: info@debrettancestry.co.uk
Website: www.debrettancestry.co.uk

# CONTENTS

# Overview

The use of surnames in England began in the Norman period, when surnames were not necessarily hereditary but usually a form of description. Some described the individual's trade or profession; others were nicknames; some gave the father's Christian name; others gave the individual's place of residence or origin.

Different surnames might be used in different documents, or more than one surname given in one document. Early descriptions were fairly elaborate and by the thirteenth and fourteenth centuries these were simpler, but still variable, and indeed the instability of surnames continued until well into the seventeenth century.

Although some Normans would already have had hereditary surnames on their arrival in Britain, the passing on of a surname from generation to generation only became customary in Britain gradually during the course of the thirteenth and fourteenth centuries. At the end of this period most of the population apparently had surnames.

Variations in the spelling of a family's surname continue to be found until the present century. Before this, as most people could not read or write, the parish clerk or other official would write down the name as they heard it.

There are four main groups of surnames:

A      Local names, which describe a person by his place of residence or origin.

B      Occupational names, which describe a person by his trade or profession.

C      Surnames of relationship, which refer to the Christian name of the father or other important relative.

D      Nicknames or sobriquets, coined to describe a person in terms of his appearance or character.

Many surnames have uncertain origins, but it is generally thought that the name Sparke (which in this report is treated together with its variant Sparks, Spark and Sparkes) falls into Category D.

# Origins and Early Examples

P H Reaney's authoritative *Dictionary of English Surnames* (3rd edition, 1995, updated by R M Wilson) states that the surname Sparke derives from the Old Norse word *sparkr* or *spræk*, meaning lively or sprightly; in modern usage, the word 'sparky' probably has much the same meaning. Given its Old Norse connections, we would expect to find the earliest examples in the Danelaw counties, and Reaney gives three early examples of the surname, from Lincolnshire, Suffolk and Yorkshire, all of which fell within the Danelaw:

> William Sperc (Lincolnshire Assizes, [1] 1202)
> Ralph Sparke (Suffolk, 1221)[2]
> John Sparkes (Yorkshire Subsidy Rolls, 1301)[3]

Hank and Hodges' *Dictionary of Surnames* (1992), which has broader geographic scope, adopts Reaney's derivation for the English surname Sparke but also notes that the surname appears in Low German as a cognate of Sparrow, with variants Spahr and Spaar. Hanks and

---

[1] Assizes were court sessions which tried the more serious crimes and were presided over by judges on circuit in England and Wales. The sort of cases they tried were capital and other serious offences such as murder, rape, robbery, burglary and arson *etc*. These courts remained in use until 1876.

[2] *Index to the Charters & Rolls in the British Museum* (London 1902), 2 vols, the Tiberius volume.

[3] The Subsidy Rolls was a tax levied on possessions rather than land, but not all householders were included in this tax. If they were too poor to be taxed or only had possessions that were necessary to their work, they would be exempt.

3

Hodges list the forms Sprake, Sprague and Spragg(e) as variants of the English name Sparke. Reaney treats the surname Spragg as a separate but related entity, with the variants Spragge, Sprague and Sprake, which he explains:

> *Sprag* is a voiced form of *sprak*, a metathesis of *spark*.
> cf Wiltshire dialect – *sprack* 'lively'

Three fourteenth century examples of this form are given by Reaney:

| | |
|---|---|
| Reginald Sprag | Suffolk Feudal Aids, 1303[4] |
| Richard Sprak | Suffolk Subsidy Rolls, 1327 |
| Alice Sprakes | Somerset, 1359[5] |

For the purposes of this study we have concentrated on the surname Sparke *etc* but have also noted any entries for Sprag, Sprake *etc*.

C W Bardsley's earlier *Dictionary of English and Welsh Surnames with Special American Instances* (1967) includes a wide range of sources including nineteenth century directories. Bardsley rather unconvincingly suggests that the surname Sparke was derived from the personal name or nickname *Sperhauke* (or similar), meaning 'Sparrowhawk'. He cites the following medieval examples, among others, which clearly relate to 'Sparrowhawk':

| | |
|---|---|
| Nicholas Sparke | Hundred Rolls, Norfolk 1273 |

---

[4] *Inquisitions and Assessments relating to Feudal Aids* 6 volumes (London 1899–1921).

[5] B H Putnam, *The Enforcement of the Statutes of Labourers 1349-1359* (New York, 1908).

Robertus Spark          Poll Tax, Yorkshire 1379

Magota Spark            Poll Tax, Yorkshire 1379

The Victorian surname dictionary *Patronymica Brittanica* (1860)[6] gives a less scholarly account of the surname Sparke but raises the possibility of a connection with two place-names:

> Spark, Sparke, Sparkes, Sparks – I think the former two must represent an old personal name – the latter two its genitive form. Sparkford and Sparkenhow, names of places, may be from the same source.

Eilert Ekwall's *Oxford Dictionary of English Place-Names* (4th edition, 1987) contains no entry for the place name Sparkenhow but includes two incidences of the place-name Sparkford:

### Sparkford, Hampshire near Winchester
| | | |
|---|---|---|
| 1212 | *Sparkeford* | Fees[7] |
| 1311 | *Sparkeford* | Inquisition Post Mortem |

### Sparkford, Somerset
| | | |
|---|---|---|
| 1086 | *Spercheford* | Domesday Book |
| 1086 | *Sparkeforda* | Domesday Book |
| 1242 | *Sperkeford* | Fees |

A surname *atte Sperke* 1333 Subs[idy Rolls] Do[rset] is mentioned in the *Place- Names of Devon*. There must have been an Old English *spearca* or *spearce* with some sense that rendered it liable to enter into place names. Such a word would belong to [the] Old English [word] *spræc* 'shoot, twig', *spracen* 'Rhamnus

---

[6] This is still of value, and was the 'endeavour' of M A Lower.

[7] *The Book of Fees Rolls Service* (1920–1931).

frangula', Norwegian *sprake* 'juniper', Old Norse *sprek,* 'dry twig'. The probability is that the word had a meaning such as 'brushwood', or else denoted some particular tree or shrub.

There certainly was an Old English word *spearca*; it appears in Aelfric's *Life of King Oswald* (ca 998) and means 'spark'. Quite how might come to be an element in place-names is less clear and as Ekwall speculates, there might have been another meaning for the word, or a similar word, that had some topographical sense.

Ekwall also identifies another early surname reference from Dorset in 1333: *atte Sperke.* The source of Ekwall's reference is the English Place-Names Society's work on Devon[8] (PND) under the place-name Sparkwell (Staverton parish), which appears in the Domesday Book (1086) as *Sperchewilla.* The editors conclude that the (Old English) word *spearca* (spark) was in use as a personal name or nickname, but the isolated example *atte Sperke* (which is from Dorset) suggest that the same word or a similar one might have had a topographical sense.

The PND also identifies Sparke's Farm in Axminster Hundred, near Upottery. This provides another medieval example of the surname *Sperke*, from Devon:

Hawis' Sperke (1330 Devon Subsidy Rolls)

*The Place-Names of Devon* also deals with the place-name Sparkhayne, confirming the supposition of M A Lower

---

[8] J E B Gover, A Mawer & F M Stenton (editors) *The Place-Names of Devon,* 2 vols (Cambridge, 1932), vol 2, pages 520–21; 650–51.

in his *Patronymica Britannica* that a personal medieval name Sparke (or a variant thereof) gave rise to place-names of this type. Sparkhayne is in the hundred of Bampton, Devon, and early forms were as follows:

| | |
|---|---|
| *Sperkeheghe* | 1311 Assize Rolls (Devon) |
| *Spearkeheghes* | 1356 Assize Rolls (Devon) |

These are relatively late examples, however, and so could derive from a surname rather than a given name: we do not have any evidence of a given name Spark or similar but this may be inferred from the early forms of some place-names.

To conclude, these investigations of the medieval evidence – which is naturally patchy – point to a single etymological source (the word meaning 'lively') which has found its way into both surnames and place-names. There may however have been another source, or sources, such as a topographical word or a personal name, for which we have no firm evidence but which may be inferred from some of the examples shown.

# Distribution

As we have seen, the element 'Spark' *etc* is found in several Devon place-names. David Postle's *The Surnames of Devon* (1995) is the only one of the six publications of the English Surnames Series to include it as a surname. Under the section dealing with the hereditary surnames of serfs, Postle cites a bond tenant at Berry Pomeroy in the reign of Edward I (1272–1307) named William Dulle Sparke ('evidently a nickname') and another, presumably his son, named William Dulle Sparkson; this is a good example of a byname becoming a hereditary surname. In the same parish in the 1290s there was a burgess named William Sparke and another customary tenant who was recorded as William *filius Willelmi Sparke*.

The surname Sparke also appears in Devon criminal records dated 1238[9] when Robert Sparke was abducted by Amadas de Wike and Walter de Wyke over the county border to Killigorrick. The Place-Name Society volume for Devon also mentions this Robert Sparke and suggests that it was his family that gave rise to the place-name Sparkaton in the parish of Meavy.

H R Moulton's *Palaeography, Genealogy and Topography*, primarily a sale catalogue printed in the 1930s, lists miscellaneous historical documents, ancient charters, leases, court rolls *etc*, and is a useful though haphazard

---

[9] *Crown Pleas Devon* 1238.

source of early surname references. We found here several entries for the surname Sparks *etc* as follows:

**14 July 1491**
Grant by Thomas Bunnyng of Hardewyk and John Bunnyng of Pulham to John Bunnyng the elder, of Denton, Thomas Spark, Thomas Webster of Tasburgh, Robert Fraunceys of Pulham, Richard Love of Pulham and Thomas Warde of Redynhale of three pieces of land in Hardewyke in an enclosure called Watergate. Witnesses: Richard Moor, Thomas Wolnawe, Richard Peyntow, John Moore of Shelton and William Warde of Pulham (stained) Fragment of seal

**1505-1597**
Sparke family. A collection of 8 charters 1505 to 1597, relating to Sparke of Dunsford, Bridford etc county Devon

**12 May 1543**
Indenture of demise by Alice Lanyan, widow and William Hammond, gentleman to Robert Sperke, of a close called Waterlete Marshe, a close called Counties Marshe and land called the Lytell Allers in Weke, Brydford, County Devon.
Signature of William Hammond

**4 February 1563**
Bargain and sale by John Servyngton (signature) of Langford, Wiltshire to Robert Sparke of lands in Dunsford, county Devon

**8 February 1563**
Grant by John Servington esquire of Langford county Wiltshire, to Robert Sparke, husbandman, of Dunsford county Devon, of a messuage [a house and the ground around it] and land in the same
Signature of grantor

9

**18 March 1575**
Indenture of lease by Edmond Drewe, gentleman of Hayne alias Norton in St Syres Newton county Devon to Nicholas Sperke, yeoman of Dunsford county Devon of five parcels of land, part of the Barton of Wike in Brydford, County Devon for 75 years at 13s 4d rent. Signature of lessor

**20 October 1575**
Devonshire. Hemioc. Bargain and Sale. Charles Ford and William Jervis both of Hemiock To Robert Ford.
Witnesses: Nicholas Marsh, Wyll Robynson, John Ford, Nycholas Sprake.
Signatures: Charlys Ford, Wyllyam Gervys 2 seals

**9 December 1577**
Assignment of lease of the capital messuage called Wyke Barten in Bridford, county Devon by Edmund Drewe to Nicholas Sparke of Dunsford

**6 April 1588**
Quit claim by Nicholas and John Holman, sons of William Holman, husbandman, of Bridford, county Devon, to Nicholas Sperke, yeoman of Dunsford, county Devon, of their interest in a tenement called Shepen and Coldharbor in Bridford.
Two marks

**4 October 1588**
Assignment of Bartholomew Northmoore to Nicholas Sparke of a lease of lands in Bridford, Devon.

**2 November 1593**
Bond of John Williams, gentleman, to Nicholas Spark of Dunsford, county Devon, yeoman in £200 the condition being that if Nicholas Sparks shall hold a messuage and lands in Weeke and Bridford, county

Devon (which he purchased from Edmond Drewe, gentleman) without any hindrance from John Williams, then this deed shall be void.

Witnesses: Rob Rowdon, mark of Robert Drake, mark of Thomas Gotham, John Sanders

Signature: Jo Williams

### 3 October 1599

Indenture of lease by Nicholas Sparke, yeoman, of Dunsford, county Devon to Marie Tottle [sic], wife of Henry Tottell esquire of Peamour and daughter of the said Nicholas and Jeffery and Johanne Tottell son and daughter of Henry and Marie of a messuage called Winscombe with two griste mills and two tuckinge or fullinge mills in Dunsford for 21 years at the yearly rent of 16s. Mark of lessor

### 20 February 1611

Indenture of grant by William Stockman of Bereford county Wiltshire esquire and John Good of Easte Tytherley, county Hampshire, gentleman, to James Sparcke of Barkeley, county Somerset, gentleman, for £400 of a messuage *etc* and land called Mervins alias Martyns in Norton Bavonte, county Wiltshire, late in the tenure of John Dewe part of the possessions of the late monastery of Dertford. Attorneys to deliver seisin: Robert Hippesley and Thomas Kettle

Signed: William Stockman, John Good. Seal. Endorsed with note of enrolment in the King's Bench, Easter Term 9 James 1 roll 186

### 28 September 1652

Lease by Peter Courtenay of Trethurffe, Jonathan Raishleigh of Menabilly, Henry Spoure of Trebarth, Jonathan Sparke of Plymouth, and Thomas Hoblyn to Walter Vincent of Tregarvethan of lands in the manor of Trevennell in St Just *etc* county Cornwall

**6 March 1663**
Bond. John Servyngton of Langford, county Wiltshire, esquire. To Robert Sparke of Dunsford, county Devon, husbandman, in £1000 for the observance etc of a pair of indentures dated 4 February 1662/3 and made between the above parties.

**10 May 1736**
Assignment. Dartmouth, *etc*. John Hill of Trevethick, county Cornwall, Arthur Holdsworth of Dartmouth, Marcella his wife, George Prideaux of Kingsbridge, county Devon, the said John, Marcella and George being residuary legatees of Walter Jago, late of Dartmouth, deceased. To Henry Holdsworth of Dartmouth. Witnesses: William Beavis, Ro Sparke
Signature of John Hill, Arthur Holdsworth, Marcella Holdsworth, George Prideaux. Four armorial seals.

Most of these documents relate to the Spark(e)(s) family of Dunsford, Devon, and show how a surname was liable to change from document to document. Nicholas Sparks was recorded as Sperke in March 1575 and April 1588, Sparke in December 1577, October 1588 and October 1599, and Spark in November 1593. He was also quite likely to be the Nicholas Sprake of the October 1575 deed. A later generation of the family at Dunsford appear to have settled on the name as Sparke.

Bardsley (see above) noted the following appearances of the name Sparke and variants in three nineteenth century directories, one of them from America:

**West Riding of Yorkshire Court Directory 1867**
Spark:      2
Sparke:     1
Sparks:     0
Sparkes:    0

**London Commercial Directory 1870**

Spark:      4
Sparke:     1
Sparks:     26
Sparkes:    3

**Jas Gopsill & Sons,** *Philadelphia* **1885**

Spark:      1
Sparke:     0
Sparks:     51
Sparkes:    0

This indicates that by the latter half of the nineteenth century the form Sparks was dominant.

This is confirmed by the 1871 census indexes provided by *Ancestry.co.uk,* which show the following statistics for the surname (in England only) in its various forms:

Sparke:     615
Sparks:     3193
Spark:      891
Sparkes:    1734

These indexes also indicate that Devon was no longer the dominant area of concentration of the surname, but a full analysis of census data has not been carried out.

In 1890 H B Guppy published his *Homes of Family Names in Great Britain,* still the only published work on surname distribution in Britain as a whole. His work was based on printed genealogies and a survey of county directories for the 1880s, in which he looked especially at the names of farmers, reasoning that they were among the most stable groups in society. Guppy restricted his study to names which appeared in a proportion of seven in 10,000 or higher:

| Sparkes | Devon | 14:10,000 |
|---------|-------|-----------|
| Sparks | Devon | 7:10,000 |
| | Somerset | 9:10,000 |
| Sprake | Dorset | 31:10,000 |

Sparke was the name of a gentle family of Plymouth in the 16th and 17th centuries: John Sparke was mayor of Plymouth in 1583. Sparke was the name of two Ashburton Churchwardens in the reign of Elizabeth [1558-1603]. Sparks is now the usual form of the name in Devon and Somerset.

Sparkes was the name of the incumbent of Middleton (Sussex) in the reign of Charles II [1660-1685].

Again the name Sparke(s) and Sparks was found in Devon and Sparks had spread to Somerset in sufficient enough numbers to appear in Guppy's work. We also noted the surname Sprake appearing in Dorset in large numbers.

George F Black's *The Surnames of Scotland* (1966) shows that the surname was found in Scotland by the fifteenth century:

**Spark**
1407    John Sperk, admitted burgess of Aberdeen[10]
1408    William Sperk, Aberdeen[11]
1472    John Sperk, tenant of Lytyl Perth[12]

---

[10] *Miscellany of the New Spalding Club, Aberdeen 1890–1908.*

[11] P J Anderson *Charters and other writs of the royal burgh of Aberdeen* (Aberdeen, 1890).

[12] Rev Charles Rogers *Rental Book of Cupar-Angus* (London 1879–80).

1532   Adam Spark, monk of Kilwinning[13]
1539   James Spark, admitted burgess of Aberdeen[14]
1698   Andrew Spark, merchant in Irvine[15]

Sprague From English dialectal *spag, sprak* (ON *spæk-r*, lively, active) alert, lively, intelligent

T J & Prys Morgan's *Welsh Surnames* (1985) and Edward MacLysaght's *The Surnames of Ireland* (1973) and *Guide to Irish Surnames* (1965) do not include Sparke (*etc*). J J Kneen in *Manx Personal Names* (1937) found an entry for the surname in the parish registers of the Isle of Man in 1793 and like Bardsley assumed an origin from 'sparrowhawk'.

Many of the sources available for charting surname distribution through the centuries are necessarily confined to the wealthier sectors of the population: in general, nobody wanted to know the names of the poor but the names of those with money or land were naturally of interest to the authorities. However, one source that covers the whole of the social spectrum is provided by English parish registers, the earliest of which began in 1538 following a mandate that all parish priests should keep a weekly record of all baptisms, marriages and burials that took place in their parish. A pre-internet survey of a cross section of parish registers for the years 1601 and 1602 was carried out in 1910 by F K and S Hitching; incidences of a particular surname are noted by parish and county, although with no indication of numbers of references.

---

[13] *Liber collegii Nostre Domine registrum ecclesie B V Marie at Anne infra muros civitatis Glasguensis MDXLIX* (Glasgow, 1846).
[14] *Miscellany of the New Spalding Club, Aberdeen 1890–1908.*
[15] J S Dobie *Muniments of the royal burgh of Irvine* (Edinburgh, 1890–91).

In the volume dealing with the registers of 1601 only one entry was found: Sparke appeared in the parish registers of North Elham in Norfolk. In 1602, further entries were found across a wider area, but again restricted to the south-east of England:

| | |
|---|---|
| Sparke | St Christopher le Stocks, London & Brundish, Suffolk |
| Sparkes | Lee, Kent |
| Sparks | Datchworth, Hertfordshire |
| Spragge | St Martin in the Fields, London |

Modern online indexes of parish registers naturally provide much broader (though not complete) coverage. A search of the *FamilySearch* index to baptisms recorded in English parish registers in the first half-century of their existence (1538–1588) brings up a list of 1640 items for the name Sparke (without variants) but this index contains a large number of duplicate entries. 216 of these entries are from Devon parishes; 85 are from London; 72 from Norfolk; 51 from Cheshire; 41 from Surrey; 36 from Lincolnshire; 31 from Worcestershire; 27 from Cornwall; 26 from Wiltshire; 23 from Suffolk; 21 from Middlesex (some of which overlap with the London list) 19 from Hertfordshire; 16 from Westmorland (including duplicates); 14 from Yorkshire; 14 from Kent; 13 from Gloucestershire; 10 from Buckinghamshire; 8 from Essex; 7 from Staffordshire (including 3 obvious duplicates); 7 from County Durham; 3 (with one obvious duplicate) from Hertfordshire; 1 from Berkshire. No entries are shown in this period from the counties of Cumberland, Northumberland, Hampshire, Herefordshire, Northamptonshire, Leicestershire, Shropshire, Warwickshire, Lancashire or Sussex. Thus, while this gives only a general picture, since the coverage of counties is not even, Devon stands out as the major home of the surname Sparke at this period.

Another useful guide to the distribution of surnames for the sixteenth, seventeenth and eighteenth centuries in England is provided by the indexes to wills proved, and administrations granted, at the Prerogative Court of (the Archbishop of) Canterbury, in London, which had superior jurisdiction over local ecclesiastical courts where wills were proved until 1858. The PCC thus provides a national index, although it is not a completely representative one, as testators whose wills were proved in the PCC were mostly among the wealthier members of society, and a disproportionate number of them were from London or Middlesex. Devon, and the other counties which were a long way from the metropolis, are generally not strongly represented.

A search of the printed PCC indexes for the years 1558 to 1583; 1584 to 1604; 1605 to 1619; 1620 to 1629; 1653 to 1656; 1657 to 1660; 1661 to 1670; 1671 to 1675; 1676 to 1685; 1686 to 1693; 1694 to 1700; 1701 to 1749; and 1750 to 1800 found the following entries for the surname:

**1558-1599**

| | | |
|---|---|---|
| Devon | Sparke | 1 |
| Lincolnshire | Spark | 1 |
| London | Sparke | 1 |
| Somerset | Spark | 1 |
| | Sparke | 3 |
| Suffolk | Sparke | 2 |

**Seventeenth Century**

| | | |
|---|---|---|
| Bedfordshire | Sparke | 1 |
| Berkshire | Sparke | 1 |
| Buckinghamshire | Sparke | 1 |

|                      |         |   |
|----------------------|---------|---|
|                      | Sparkes | 1 |
|                      | Sparks  | 1 |
| Cheshire             | Sparke  | 1 |
| Devon                | Sparck  | 1 |
|                      | Spark   | 1 |
|                      | Sparke  | 5 |
|                      | Sperke  | 1 |
| County Durham        | Sparke  | 2 |
| Essex                | Sparke  | 4 |
|                      | Sparkes | 1 |
| Flintshire           | Sparke  | 1 |
| Gloucestershire      | Sparke  | 1 |
| Hertfordshire        | Sparke  | 2 |
|                      | Sparkes | 1 |
| Kent                 | Sparke  | 2 |
|                      | Sparkes | 4 |
| London               | Sparke  | 7 |
|                      | Sparkes | 6 |
|                      | Sparks  | 1 |
| Middlesex            | Sparke  | 4 |
|                      | Sparkes | 5 |
| Norfolk              | Spark   | 1 |
|                      | Sparke  | 7 |
| Oxfordshire          | Sparkes | 1 |
| *Pts* (Foreign Parts) | Sparke  | 2 |
|                      | Sparkes | 4 |
|                      | Sparks  | 1 |
| Somerset             | Spark   | 1 |
|                      | Sparke  | 2 |
| Suffolk              | Spark   | 1 |
|                      | Sparke  | 4 |
| Surrey               | Sparke  | 5 |
|                      | Sparkes | 5 |
| Warwickshire         | Spark   | 1 |

The PCC was used for testators who died abroad and we have seven examples of people named Spark *etc* who died overseas. The most common variants found for this period were Sparke and Sparkes, with the highest appearance of the name, in its various forms, again found in the south-east of England.

**1700-1750**

| | | |
|---|---|---|
| Berkshire | Sparks | 1 |
| Buckinghamshire | Sparkes | 4 |
| Cambridge | Sparke | 1 |
| Cornwall | Sparke | 2 |
| Derbyshire | Sparks | 1 |
| Devon | Sparke | 1 |
| | Sparks | 1 |
| Essex | Sparke | 1 |
| Gloucestershire | Sparkes | 2 |
| Hertfordshire | Sparkes | 2 |
| Kent | Sparkes | 2 |
| | Sparks | 1 |
| Lincolnshire | Sparkes | 2 |
| London | Sparke | 8 |
| | Sparkes | 8 |
| Middlesex | Sparke | 12 |
| | Sparkes | 12 |
| | Sparks | 3 |
| Northamptonshire | Sparkes | 3 |
| Oxfordshire | Sparke | 2 |
| | Sparkes | 2 |
| *Pts* | Sparke | 3 |
| | Sparkes | 9 |
| | Sparks | 7 |
| Suffolk | Sparke | 2 |
| Surrey | Sparke | 2 |
| | Sparkes | 1 |
| | Sparks | 1 |
| Sussex | Sparkes | 1 |
| | Sparks | 1 |

19

As expected, high numbers were found for London and Middlesex and for those persons dying overseas. However, the name does not appear to be as highly concentrated in the south-east during this period, but has spread fairly evenly throughout the country.

**1751-1800**

| | | |
|---|---|---|
| Buckinghamshire | Sparks | 1 |
| Cambridgeshire | Sparkes | 1 |
| Cornwall | Spark | 1 |
| | Sparke | 1 |
| Devon | Sparke | 3 |
| | Sparks | 2 |
| Dorset | Sparke | 2 |
| | Sparks | 2 |
| Essex | Sparkes | 1 |
| | Sparks | 1 |
| Gloucestershire | Sparke | 1 |
| | Sparkes | 1 |
| Hertfordshire | Sparkes | 2 |
| | Sparks | 1 |
| Kent | Spark | 1 |
| | Sparke | 1 |
| | Sparkes | 4 |
| | Sparks | 1 |
| London | Sparke | 1 |
| | Sparkes | 2 |
| | Sparks | 1 |
| Middlesex | Spark | 2 |
| | Sparke | 3 |
| | Sparkes | 8 |
| | Sparks | 7 |
| Northamptonshire | Sparke | 3 |
| Pts | Spark | 4 |
| | Sparke | 1 |
| | Sparkes | 2 |
| | Sparks | 6 |

| Somerset | Sparks | 2 |
|---|---|---|
| Staffordshire | Sparkes | 1 |
| Suffolk | Spark | 1 |
| | Sparke | 1 |
| | Sparkes | 1 |
| Surrey | Sparkes | 4 |
| | Sparks | 3 |

Again Middlesex is well represented by Spark *etc* testators, but we can also see that the name has spread even further across the country and more variants of the name are represented here during this period.

For the nineteenth century, H B Guppy's survey has been mentioned above. Another important Victorian source is the *Return of Owners of Land* of 1873, sometimes known as the Modern Domesday Book. This source lists, county by county, every owner of an acre of land or more, with their residence (not necessarily the address of their property) and the acreage of their holding.

**Return of Owners of Land**

| Bedfordshire | 1 | Sparks |
|---|---|---|
| Brecknockshire | 1 | Sparks |
| Cambridgeshire | 2 | Spark |
| | 3 | Sparke |
| | 1 | Sparks |
| Cardiganshire | 1 | Sparks |
| Cheshire | 2 | Sparks |
| Cumberland | 1 | Spark |
| Devon | 1 | Spark |
| | 4 | Sparke |
| | 4 | Sparkes |
| | 5 | Sparks |
| Dorset | 1 | Sparkes |
| County Durham | 3 | Spark |
| Essex | 5 | Sparks |

| | | |
|---|---|---|
| Gloucestershire | 2 | Sparkes |
| | 2 | Sparks |
| Hampshire | 2 | Sparkes |
| Kent | 1 | Sparks |
| Leicestershire | 1 | Sparke |
| Middlesex | 1 | Sparkes |
| | 2 | Sparks |
| Monmouthshire | 1 | Sparkes |
| | 1 | Sparks |
| Norfolk | 2 | Sparke |
| | 2 | Sparkes |
| | 2 | Sparks |
| Northamptonshire | 1 | Sparke |
| Northumberland | 1 | Spark |
| | 3 | Sparke |
| Salop | 1 | Sparkes |
| Somerset | 1 | Spark |
| | 3 | Sparkes |
| | 9 | Sparks |
| Staffordshire | 1 | Sparkes |
| Suffolk | 6 | Sparke |
| | 3 | Sparkes |
| | 1 | Sparks |
| Surrey | 6 | Sparkes |
| Sussex | 3 | Sparkes |
| Warwickshire | 1 | Sparkes |
| Wiltshire | 2 | Sparks |

The surname Sparke appears in most of the English counties with one appearance, each, of Sparks in Brecknockshire and Cardiganshire; as we know that this is not a Welsh surname, these Sparks were, no doubt, migrants from England.

# Famous bearers of the name

The *Dictionary of National Biography* (1975 edition) for the British Isles has entries for the following people named Sparke *etc*:

> Thomas Spark DD (1655-1692) – classical scholar
> Edward Sparke (d 1692) – divine
> Joseph Sparke(s) (1683-1740) – antiquarian
> Thomas Sparke (1548-1616) – divine

For the more modern period, Debrett's *People of Today* (1999) includes entries for the following:

> Muriel Spark DBE (born 1918) - author
> David Sparkes (born 1946) – designer
> John Jackson Sparkes (born 1924) – professor
> Ian Leslie Sparks (born 1943) – social worker
> (Robert) Stephen John Sparks (born 1949) – professor

There are many coats of arms listed in Burke's *General Armory* granted to men of the name Sparke *etc*. Several of these belong to subsidiary branches of a single family, from Nantwich in Cheshire, but there are other entries from London, Devon and elsewhere:

> **Spark** – argent on a bend sable a rose of the field.

> **Spark or Sparke** – Vert and eagle displayed ermine. Crest – A swan in pride devouring a fish proper

> **Sparke** (Nantwich, county Chester) – Chequy or and vert, a bend ermine. Crest – Out of a ducal coronet or, a demi panther rampant guardant argent spotted with various colours, fire issuing form the ears and mouth proper

**Sparke** (London, and county Essex, 1577) – Same Arms and Crest

**Sparke** (Jersey, the heiress married John Payne of St Martin's Jersey) – Same Arms and Crest

**Sparke** (Plimpton St Maurice and Plymouth county Devon; John Sparke of Plymouth, Visitation Cornwall 1620, son of John Sparke, of same place, and grandson of John Spearke, of Plimpton, who came from Nantwich) – Same Arms and Crest, an annulet gules for difference

**Sparke** (Gunthorpe Hall, county Norfolk) – Chequy or and vert, a fess ermine. Crest – Out of a ducal coronet or, a demi panther rampant guardant argent spotted with various colours, fire issuing out of the ears and mouth proper

**Sparke** – Azure an eagle displayed argent membered or

**Sparke** (Funeral Entry Ulster's Office, 1596, Joane Sparke, wife of Stephen Segrave, Keeper of the Crane of Dublin, who were both blown up by the bursting of a barrel of gunpowder) – Chequy or and Azure a bend ermine

**Sparke** (Sir William Sparke, one of the Justices of the King's Bench; funeral entry, Ulster's office, 1623) – Chequy sable and or a bend ermine

**Sparkes** (county Cornwall, and Plymouth, county Devon) – Chequy or and vert, a bend ermine, a label with three points gules. Crest – Out of a ducal coronet or a demi lion guttée de sang[16]

**Sparkes** (Glenham, county Suffolk ) – Chequy or and vert, a bend ermine. Crest – a fleur-de-lis or

**Sparkes** (Pennyworlodd Hall, county Brecon) – Chequy or and vert, a bend ermine. Crest – out of a ducal coronet or, a demi panther rampant guardant argent spotted with various colours, fire issuing form the ears and mouth proper

**Sparks** (Byfleet, county Surrey; formerly seated in county Wexford) – Chequy or and vert, a bend ermine. Crest – Out of a ducal coronet or, a demi panther rampant guardant and spotted with various colours, fire issuing from the ears and mouth proper

---

[16] *Guttée de sang* - signifying that the field was strewn with drops of blood (red).

# Printed Genealogies

We have found the following references to printed genealogies of families bearing this name:

### Sparke
*Visitations of Berkshire* (Harleian Society) lvi, 286
*Visitations of Cheshire* (Harleian Society) lix, 217
J L Vivian *Visitations of Devon* 856
*Cheshire Visitations Pedigrees 1663* (Harleian Society) xciii, 101
Ruvigny *The Plantagenet Roll of the Blood Royal: The Mortimer-Percy Volume* (1911) 423
J B Payne *Roll of the High Sheriffs of England and Wales for the year 1877* (1878) 57
*Genealogist's Magazine* v, 75
E Powell *Pedigree of the Families of Powell and Baden-Powell* (1926) 43
J G Brooker *Pedigrees* (1942-3) 82
W Rye *Norfolk Families* (1915) 822
Burke's *Landed Gentry* 1868, 1871, 1875, 1879, 1952
*Harleian Society* ix, 205; xvii, 256
*The Genealogist* vi, 94
Howard *Visitations of England and Wales, notes* iii, 54

### Sparkes
Burke's *Landed Gentry* 1846-8, 1860, 1863, 1868
*The Midland Antiquary* ii, 95

### Sparks
Burke's *Landed Gentry* 1846-8, 1860, 1863
*The Pedigree Register* (1907-16) i, 88
R E Tickell *The Tickell and Connected Families: Fairfax, Eustace etc* (1948) 56
F A Crisp *Visitations of England and Wales* (1895)

*Miscellanea Genealogica et Heraldica* New Series ii, 469
Howard *Visitation of England and Wales* iii, 126

# Summary

To conclude, the name Sparke (with its principal variants Spark, Spark(e)s) probably derives in many instances, as suggested by P H Reaney, as a nickname from the Old Norse adjective *sparkr* or *spræk* meaning lively or sprightly. The earliest examples found are from the Danelaw area (Yorkshire, Lincolnshire, Norfolk, Suffolk), which supports this theory. However, by 1330 we find it in Devon, far from the Danelaw. Here it is possibly related to the Old English noun *spearca* (spark) which might have been used as a nickname, but the place-name evidence suggests that there might have been a similar word, or a different meaning of the same word, of a topographical nature. From the early modern period the surname appears to have been concentrated in Devon. We have also found evidence that a family of this name was well established in Suffolk from an early date.

# Sources Consulted

P H Reaney, *The Origins of English Surnames* (London: Routledge & Kegan Paul, 1967)

P H Reaney & R M Wilson, *A Dictionary of British Surnames* (Oxford: Oxford University Press, 3rd edition, 1995)

P H Reaney, *Dictionary of British Surnames* (London: Routledge & Kegan Paul, 2nd edition, 1976)

P Hanks & F Hodges, *A Dictionary of Surnames* (Oxford University Press, 1988)

M A Lower, *Patronymica Brittanica* (London, 1860)

C W Bardsley, *Dictionary of English and Welsh Surnames* (1901: reprinted, Baltimore: Genealogical Publishing Co, 1967)

C L'Estrange Ewen, *Guide to the Origin of British Surnames* (London: John Gifford, 1938)

H B Guppy, *Homes of Family Names in Great Britain* (London, 1890)

Ernest Weekley, *The Romance of Names* (London: John Murray, 2nd edition, 1917)

Ernest Weekley, *Surnames* (London: John Murray, 1917)

George F Black, *The Surnames of Scotland* (New York Public Library, 1946)

Edward McLysaght, *The Surnames of Ireland* (Dublin: Irish University Press, 1977)

T J & Prys Morgan, *Welsh Surnames* (Cardiff: University of Wales Press, 1985)

F K & S Hitching, *References to English Surnames in 1601* (Walton on Thames: Bernau, 1910)

F K & S Hitching, *References to English Surnames in 1602* (Walton on Thames: Bernau, 1911)

*Debrett's People of Today* (Debrett's Peerage Limited: London, 1996)

*The Dictionary of National Biography: Index & Epitome* (London, 1906)

*The Concise Dictionary of National Biography*, Part II, 1901–1950, (Oxford, 1961)

*Burke's Family Index* (London: Burke's Peerage Limited, 1976)

H R Moulton, *Palaeography, Genealogy & Topography* (Sale Catalogue, 1930)

Index to Prerogative Court of Canterbury Wills (The National Archives: online)

G W Marshall, *The Genealogist's Guide* (1903; reprinted, Baltimore: GPC 1973)

J B Whitmore, *A Genealogical Guide* (London, 1953)

Charles Bridge, *An Index to Pedigrees* (London, 1867)

Geoffrey B Barrow, *The Genealogist's Guide* (London: Research Publishing Co, 1977)

Sir Bernard Burke, *The General Armory* (London, 1884)

C R Humphrey-Smith, editor, *Burke's General Armory Volume II*, (Tabard Press, 1973)

*The Return of Owners of Land* (1873)

Eilert Ekwall, *The Concise Oxford Dictionary of English Place-Names* (Oxford: Clarendon Press, 4th edition, 1960)

E G Withycombe, *The Oxford Dictionary of English Christian Names* (Oxford: Clarendon Press, 2nd edition, 1950)

W J Hardy & W Page, *A Calendar to the Feet of Fines for London and Middlesex: Vol 1 Richard I – Richard III (1189–1485)* (London, 1892)

Richard McKinley, *The Surnames of Oxfordshire* (English Surnames Series III: Leopard's Head Press, 1977)

Richard McKinley, *The Surnames of Sussex* (English Surnames Series V: Leopard's Head Press, 1988)

Richard McKinley, *The Surnames of Lancashire* (English Surnames Series IV: Leopard's Head Press, 1981)

Richard McKinley, *Norfolk and Suffolk Surnames in the Middle Ages* (English Surnames Series II: Phillimore, 1975)

George Redmonds, *Yorkshire West Riding* (English Surnames Series I: Phillimore, 1973)

Mr Avenell, *The Norman People* (London, 1874)

*Debrett's Heraldry* (London, 1933)

J P Brooke-Little, revised, *Boutell's Heraldry* (Frederick Warne: London, 1970)

Indexes to 1841–1911 Census Returns of England and Wales (The National Archives/*Ancestry.co.uk*)

*Sweet's Anglo-Saxon Reader in Prose and Verse* (15th edition, edited Dorothy Whitelock: Oxford, 1967)